Copyrig
Wright

MW00928414

Published by Alexander Books

Follow the author on Instagram for free book giveaways (no strings attached), free mental health information, and more:

@alexander_wright_books

This publication is designed to provide accurate and authoritative information in regard to the subject matter covered. It is sold with the

The Serotonin Book: How to Maximize Your Serotonin Levels Naturally

By

Alexander Wright

Table of Contents

Chapter 1: What is Serotonin?

Serotonin is a catecholamine molecule also referred to as 5-hydroxytryptamine (5-HT). It also has hormonal effects.

Serotonin functions as a receptor, which means it conveys signals between nerve cells in your body and central nervous system (your peripheral nervous system). Your body receives molecular instructions on how to operate.

Serotonin affects learning, memory, and pleasure in addition to controlling body temperature, slumber, appetite, and reproductive activity in your body. Serotonin deficiency is believed to contribute to hyperactivity, anxiety, depression, and other illnesses.

Your stomach contains the majority of the serotonin in your body (intestines). The cells lining your GI system contain about 90% of your body's serotonin supply. It is dispersed into your bloodstream and taken up by platelets. Your brain only produces 10% of your serotonin supply.

Tryptophan, an important amino acid, is used to make serotonin. It cannot be produced by your body, which deems it as what is known as a "necessary amino acid." It must be acquired through food or supplements.

Why does my body produce serotonin?

Serotonin is involved in a wide range of bodily processes, including:

Mood: Serotonin is a cerebral chemical that controls mood. It is frequently referred to as your body's inborn "feel happy" hormone. You feel more mentally secure, happy, relaxed, and more emotionally centered when serotonin levels are typical. Depression and low serotonin levels are related. Numerous drugs prescribed to address anxiety, depression, and other mood disorders frequently work to raise the brain's serotonin levels.

Digestion: The majority of the serotonin in your body is found in your gastrointestinal system, where it plays a part in safeguarding your stomach and controlling bowel movements. Your stomach can produce more serotonin, which will hasten metabolism and help your body get clear of unpleasant meals and harmful products. Additionally, serotonin helps you feel fuller after meals.

When serotonin is released into your stomach more quickly than it can be metabolized, nausea is the result. Numerous medications used to lessen nausea and vomiting target particular serotonin receptors in the brain.

Sleep: Serotonin and the chemical dopamine both contribute to the quality of your sleep (how well and how long you sleep). In order to create melatonin, a hormone that controls your sleep-wake pattern, your brain requires serotonin.

Wound healing: Serotonin is produced by platelets in your circulatory system to aid in the mending of lesions. Arterioles, the smallest blood arteries, constrict when there is an injury, slowing blood movement and promoting the formation of clots. This step in the mending process of any injury that causes bleeding is crucial.

Bone health: Your bone mass may be influenced by your serotonin levels. Bone fractures and osteoporosis can result from brittle bones, which can be caused by high amounts of serotonin in the stomach.

Sexual health: Dopamine and serotonin both contribute to your urge for intercourse.

What conditions are brought on by reduced serotonin levels?

Numerous health problems, including the following, may be linked to low serotonin levels:

- depression and various emotional issues
- anxiety
- issues with sleep
- digestive difficulties
- obsessive compulsive disorder
- panic disorder
- schizophrenia
- phobias

Serotonin's function in the body and how it relates to illness is still a subject of much research for scientists.

Why might serotonin levels be low?

There are typically multiple reasons for decreased serotonin levels. Strictly speaking, reduced serotonin levels result from:

- Serotonin production is insufficient.
- Serotonin isn't being utilized properly by your body. This may occur if your body doesn't produce enough serotonin receptors or if the receptors aren't functioning properly.

How can my serotonin levels be raised?

Serotonin levels can be raised by:

- Getting enough nutrients
- Increasing your physical activity
- Eating foods that increase serotonin

- Eating foods that contain tryptophan or using tryptophan supplements. Countless foods contain tryptophan, but some of the best sources include:
1. Salmon
2. Eggs
3. Cheese
4. Turkey
5. Tofu
6. Pineapples
7. Cereals
8. Seeds
9. Nuts

Tryptophan-rich meals do not inherently increase serotonin levels on their own. It's a difficult procedure. In order to produce insulin, which is required for amino acid absorption, your body requires carbs. Even if tryptophan does enter your bloodstream, it will have to outcompete other amino acids in order to reach your brain. Researchers are still looking into how consuming meals high in tryptophan may increase serotonin levels.

- Sunlight

Some individuals may develop seasonal affective disorder if they don't get enough sunshine exposure. Attempt to get 10 to 15 minutes of sunshine each day to increase vitamin D and serotonin levels. Consider using light treatment to get the necessary everyday sunshine if you reside in a place where you can't get it naturally. A light box can bought online.

- Supplements

Serotonin levels are also raised by a number of nutritional and natural remedies. These consist of:

- Probiotics
- SAMe
- Tryptophan
- Supplements made from herbs: Examples of these include ginseng, cinnamon, Syrian rue, and St. John's wort.

- Working out. Serotonin levels have been shown to rise with regular exercise. Engaging in thirty minutes of cardiovascular exercise five times per week along with two periods of weight training can dramatically increase serotonin levels.

Which drugs raise serotonin levels?

Since serotonin affects a wide range of medical problems, serotonin or serotonin receptors are frequently targeted by the pharmaceutical business.

Antidepressants of various types prevent serotonin from being recycled and aid reabsorption, enabling more to stay in the brain. Selective serotonin reuptake inhibitors, such as paroxetine (Paxil®), serotonin-norepinephrine reuptake inhibitors, such as venlafaxine (Effexor®), and tricyclic antidepressants, such as amitriptyline (Elavil®), are medications that function in this manner. Monoamine oxidase inhibitors, such as phenelzine [Nardil®], prevent the enzyme that breaks down serotonin. They are a different class of antidepressant.

Serotonin is raised by many other drugs that are used to treat a variety of illnesses. The triptan family of headache medications, narcotic painkillers, cough suppressants with dextromethorphan, and anti-nausea medications are a few of these medicines.

What issues are brought on by elevated serotonin levels?

When serotonin levels are overly elevated, a disorder known as serotonin syndrome develops. It typically occurs if you take more than one medicine that increases serotonin or when you first increase the dosage of a prescription that is known to raise serotonin levels.

Shivering, excessive perspiration, disorientation, agitation, elevated blood pressure, muscular spasms, and defecation are examples of mild symptoms. High temperature, convulsions, dizziness, and irregular heartbeats are among the severe signs.

If serotonin syndrome is serious, it can be deadly if it is not diagnosed and addressed right away.

Chapter 2: Food

Eating foods high in tryptophan relative to other amino acids (turkey, canned tuna, apples, bananas, and oats), eating foods that directly contain serotonin (kiwi, pineapple, potato, and tomato), and increasing your intake of foods high in vitamin B6 (poultry, tuna, chickpeas, and lentils) and vitamin D are all effective ways to increase serotonin levels (mushrooms, salmon, cheese, and sardines). However, if your diet is poor generally, consuming these kinds of items alone probably won't have a noticeable effect on your serotonin levels.

Let's discuss serotonin synthesis before getting into the nutrients that raise serotonin levels.

The only antecedent to serotonin is tryptophan, an amino acid that can be found in meals high in protein. Since your body cannot produce tryptophan, you must consume meals that contain it or take nutritional supplements to get it.

Most of the tryptophan consumed after absorption is taken in the small intestine, where 95% of it is then used for the kynurenine pathway, a metabolic route that is believed to be involved in some illnesses. The residual 5% can either:

- stay in the intestines after being transformed to serotonin (roughly 90% of serotonin synthesis)
- With the aid of a transport protein, penetrate the blood brain barrier (BBB) and be transformed into serotonin for use in the brain (representing 10% of serotonin synthesis).

Which Meals Increase Serotonin Levels?

It is essential to remember that tryptophan fights with other amino acids for entrance into the brain, even though consuming meals high in tryptophan has the potential to increase serotonin levels. Therefore, increasing serotonin levels in the brain simply by consuming meals rich in tryptophan may not always have the results you're looking for. The best method to increase cerebral serotonin levels is presumably to choose meals richer in tryptophan than other amino acids.

Compared to other amino acids, the following items have higher tryptophan concentrations:

- Turkey
- Chicken
- Milk
- Bread with white or whole grains
- Chocolate

- Prepared mackerel
- Peanuts
- Cheese, cheddar
- Oats
- Baked prunes
- Bananas
- Apples

Several meals are primary sources of serotonin, but since serotonin produced outside the central nervous system (CNS) is difficult to penetrate the blood-brain barrier (BBB), their effects on mood and brain activity may be minimal.

The following items contain serotonin directly:

- Bananas
- Chinese chard and chicory
- Coffee
- Garlic
- Hazelnut
- Kiwi
- Lettuce
- Nettle

- Paprika
- Exotic berry
- Pawpaw
- Pepper
- Pineapple
- Plantain
- Plum
- Pomegranate
- Potato
- Spinach
- Strawberry
- Tomato
- Viola bean
- Innate rice

Foods high in vitamin B6 (needed for the conversion of tryptophan into serotonin) and vitamin D (helps to activate an enzyme needed to produce serotonin) may also be helpful for boosting serotonin production.

Food sources for these vitamins are:

- Poultry
- Mackerel rainbow fish

- Salmon
- Salmon Herring
- Chickpeas
- Tuna
- Animal liver
- Sardines
- Potatoes
- Tilapia
- Lentils
- Flounder
- Bananas
- Milk
- Spinach Cheese
- Carrots
- Mushrooms

Do Any Diets Increase Serotonin Levels?

It may be beneficial to some degree to include items that increase serotonin levels in your dinner plan, but your overall nutritional pattern is likely more significant. Increasing your serotonin levels with certain foods will be challenging if you frequently consume foods that harm your intestines and/or encourage inflammation.

Tryptophan levels are typically greatest in vegetarian and fish-rich diets, while tryptophan levels are lowest in vegan diets. Your chance of developing depression can rise if you consume a meal lacking in tryptophan.

It has been demonstrated that various foods, in addition to their other health-promoting effects, have a beneficial effect on serotonin.

A 14-week elimination diet that included probiotics or not significantly raised serum (blood) serotonin levels. Diets that are anti-inflammatory may help increase serotonin synthesis.

People with irritable bowel syndrome have been shown to have more serotonin-producing cells in their Gastrointestinal system when they follow a reduced FODMAP diet (IBS).

Compared to other amino acids, tryptophan is more abundant in diets rich in carbohydrates, which may make it simpler for tryptophan to penetrate the BBB and be transformed to serotonin.

The key lesson is to choose a diet that best fits your body's requirements rather than one that tries to include the most items that increase serotonin. Along with many other advantages, a diet that helps you feel good and is good for your digestive health will aid in the natural creation of serotonin.

Can Supplements Increase Serotonin Levels?

Serotonin levels may also be affected by supplementing with tryptophan. Participants in a randomized controlled study who took a substance containing tryptophan reported improved brain performance. Although serotonin levels weren't explicitly tested, the researchers believed this may have been partially caused by elevated amounts.

Tryptophan supplements have been shown to enhance happiness in other trials.

How Do Serotonin Levels React to Inflammation?

In addition to altering gastrointestinal serotonin levels, inflammation in the GI system (or elsewhere in the body) also interferes with serotonin's ability to travel from the stomach to the brain via the vagus nerve.

Typically, 5% of the tryptophan in meals that contain tryptophan is converted by your body into serotonin and melatonin. However, if you have inflammation, that 5% is instead used to make inflammatory proteins (kynurenine pathway), which eventually deprives you of the neurotransmitter that makes you feel good, serotonin.

Your bodily well-being and the degree of inflammation in your body and intestines are significantly influenced by your diet. Eating a diet high in processed and refined foods (high levels of inflammatory fat, sugar, empty calories, and salt) and low in fruits and vegetables can worsen inflammation and may divert tryptophan into the kynurenine pathway, which reduces the amount of tryptophan available for the production of serotonin. Additionally, elevated levels of amino acids that contend with tryptophan for entrance into the brain are frequently found in inflammatory foods.

Probiotics may also help with serotonin levels because of their effects on the tryptophan and kynurenine pathways, according to the scant research available. Tryptophan cannot be produced by humans, but stomach bacteria can produce serotonin and tryptophan, so enhancing the intestine's bacterial population with probiotics may naturally increase serotonin.

Before a challenging test, students who consumed a probiotic beverage for eight weeks had greater feces serotonin levels, potentially as a result of how bacteria affected tryptophan biosynthesis. The ratio of kynurenine to tryptophan was considerably lowered by taking a prebiotic for eight weeks, which meant that more tryptophan was utilized in the production of serotonin. Subjects' depressive symptoms significantly improved.

Probiotics were taken for eight weeks by people with severe depressive disorder, and their amounts of kynurenine significantly decreased.

In other studies, probiotics were found to restore serotonin levels in people with diarrhea and to help increase levels of the enzymes required for serotonin synthesis.

Chapter 3: Probiotics

You know how your stomach feels when you're about to give a toast? Or the sudden loss of appetite when bad news comes? That's your brain talking to the microbiota in your gut. This is called the gut-brain axis in the scientific world.

It works in both directions. The microbiota in your gut can also send messages to your brain. Recent studies show, in fact, taking probiotics may help improve your mood and intelligence.

More research is needed to find out which probiotic strains or doses might be the most helpful, but you can still give your brain a boost by adding probiotics to your diet in a smart way.

Why are probiotics good for the brain?

Sometimes you might feel like your stomach has its own mind, and you'd be right. The enteric nervous system (ENS) is our second brain. It's our job to make the second brain think that everything is fine in the gut so that it can tell the first brain that everything is fine.

More research has been done on Lactobacillus and Bifidobacterium strains than on other strains of probiotics (specifically the L. helveticus and B. longum strains). Researchers even call these strains "psychobiotics" because they might be used as medicines. But here's what science really knows about probiotics and the connection between the brain and the gut:

B. bifidum helps make vitamins like K and B-12, which may also affect how you feel.

B. infantis helped rats feel more relaxed and helped treat irritable bowel syndrome.

L. reuteri has been shown to help mice feel less pain and can help them get more excited.

L. plantarum made mice produce a lot more serotonin and dopamine and made them less anxious when they were in a maze.

L. acidophilus may help lower cholesterol and make it easier for the body to absorb nutrients.

Rats that were given L. helveticus had less anxiety, but a 2017 study didn't find any difference.

Try all foods with probiotics: Many foods have more than one type of probiotics, not just one (although you can purchase a specific strain in pill form).

One study, which was published in the journal Frontiers of Neuroscience, showed that people with Alzheimer's disease who took probiotics (a mixture of L. acidophilus, L. casei, B. bifidum, and L. fermentum) had better memory and learning skills.

Researchers are still looking into the link between the brain and the gut and how probiotics can help. But so far, the research looks good, and you don't have to have a long-term illness to benefit from the possible brain-boosting effects.

Most probiotics are found in foods that have been fermented. That means you can easily add them to your meals. Some fermented foods include:

- sauerkraut
- kimchi
- greek yogurt
- kefir
- pickles

Everyone has a different microbiome, so don't eat them all at once. When you start eating these foods, do it slowly at first. For example, you could start with a half cup of kefir to see how your body reacts and then work your way up to a full cup.

It's not unusual to have gas, bloating, and more bowel movements at first. If you don't have stomach pain, try more foods until probiotics are a natural part of what you eat throughout the day.

When you eat probiotics on purpose, you also make a change in how you live. Natalie Rizzo, MS, RD says that when her clients add probiotics to their diet, it's usually because they care about their health and eat well. "Both of these things can definitely help your health when done together."

Rizzo knows that it might be hard for some people to eat enough probiotic foods every day. Try to get probiotics from natural sources first. If you're unable to get in enough, Rizzo suggests a probiotic pill. You can find them in stores that sell healthy foods.

Talk to your doctor about the right dose and find a trusted, reputable manufacturer. The U.S. Food and Drug Administration (FDA) doesn't keep an eye on probiotics and other supplements. There may be concerns about safety, quality, or even the way things are packed.

What are supplements, and how do they work?

Most probiotic supplements have a mix of bacteria from different species. The daily dose is between 1 billion and 10 billion colony forming units (CFUs). A mix of probiotic strains is also often found in supplements, but the brands will usually tell you which strains they have.

Start with a lower dose of CFUs and see how your body responds before working your way up to a full dose.

Tess Catlett started taking a probiotic every day to help her stomach feel better. But she started with a high dose (10 billion CFUs) and had stomach pain.

She says, "After taking it for two or three days, I got the worst stomachache I've had in years. Think of the pain of menstrual cramps mixed with the sickness of food poisoning."

But Catlett's bloating went away after she changed the amount of the probiotic she was taking and took it every day for two weeks.

Plan when to take your probiotics. When you eat is the best time to take a probiotic. A 2011 study found that the best way to keep all the benefits of probiotic supplements is to take a pill with a meal or 30 minutes before a meal, but not 30 minutes after.

Rizzo says that if you have trouble remembering to take a pill, you should link it to something you do every day. You could, for example, make it a habit to take the supplement when you brush your teeth after breakfast.

Keep in mind that the benefits to your brain may not show up for a few weeks. This might seem like a long time, but most antidepressants take the same amount of time.

Have finals coming up? Are you worried about work deadlines coming up? Your mood might drop in the days before you get your period. Or maybe you just broke up with someone or have been having a hard time lately. All of these are times when being very smart and deliberate about what you eat and how much probiotics you take in can make a huge difference.

Immune function, which is your body's ability to fight off sickness or infection, is closely linked to both probiotics and gut health. The best way to stay healthy is to take probiotics on a regular basis. But don't be afraid to take a little more when you think you'll need a little more help.

Chapter 4: Tryptophan

Some tryptophan is also turned into nicotinamide adenine dinucleotide (NAD) by the body. Because of this, tryptophan is also a food source of niacin, which is vitamin B3.

L-tryptophan and D-tryptophan are the two kinds of tryptophan. The only difference between the two types is the orientation of the molecule.

For your body to turn tryptophan into niacin, though, it needs enough iron, vitamin B6, and vitamin B2.

Tryptophan can have plenty of health benefits, but the supplement can cause a number of unpleasant side effects in people.

Most of the time, people have problems with their stomachs.

- Heartburn
- Pain in the stomach belching
- Illness and vomiting

- Diarrhea and loss of appetite
- headaches
- Sexual problems
- Dry mouth

Some of the more serious side effects that should make you stop using the drug right away are:

- lightheadedness
- blurred vision
- weak muscles
- extreme fatigue

Good for your health

The tryptophan that is naturally found in foods is good for your health in several ways. Most of these health benefits come from the potential increase of niacin and thus serotonin. Some of the benefits of having more serotonin are:

- better and healthier sleep
- relief from depression and anxiety
- better emotional health
- better ability to handle pain

Health dangers

Tryptophan that comes from food is usually safe, but some people have bad reactions to the supplement form.

The National Organization for Rare Disorders says that tryptophan supplements were linked to 37 deaths and over 1,500 cases of eosinophilia-myalgia syndrome (EMS) in the late 1980s. This is a rare disorder that affects multiple organ systems within the body, including the skin, lungs, and muscles. It often comes on quickly and all at once. It can make people sick or even kill them. Some of the signs are:

- pain or weakness in the muscles
- skin rashes
- cramping
- difficulty breathing
- fatigue

But the EMS cases were linked to a company that made tainted tryptophan supplements. Because of this, it is more likely that the health problems were caused by contamination in the supplements than by tryptophan itself.

Tryptophan can help treat the symptoms of some conditions, but it may raise your serotonin levels too much, especially if you take it with medications like:

- Antidepressants
- MAO inhibitors (MAOIs)
- Pain relievers like tramadol and meperidine
- Triptan medications for migraine

- Vough medicine with dextromethorphan

If you are taking selective serotonin reuptake inhibitors (SSRIs), you shouldn't take tryptophan supplements without first talking to your doctor. Tryptophan can make serotonin levels rise too high and cause serotonin syndrome.

Do not take tryptophan supplements if you're pregnant, trying to get pregnant, or breastfeeding.

Used often

Tryptophan is commonly used to treat insomnia and sleep disorders like sleep apnea. But there isn't enough evidence to say whether this is a good use or not. To find out if tryptophan is safe to treat any of these conditions, more research needs to be done.

It has been said that tryptophan could help ease the symptoms of premenstrual dysphoric disorder (PMDD). Some older research suggests that tryptophan may also help people stop smoking.

Chapter 5: Exercise, Sunlight, and More

For the last 4 decades, the question of how to manipulate the serotonergic system with drugs has been an important area of research in biological psychiatry, and this research has led to advances in the treatment of depression. Research on the links between different polymorphisms and depression backs up the idea that serotonin plays a role not only in treating depression but also in making people more likely to get depressed or commit suicide. Polymorphisms of the serotonin transporter have been the focus of this research, but other serotonin-related genes may also be involved. In the future, genetic research will make it easier to figure out who is more likely to get depressed.

Less thought has been put into how this information can help people who are more likely to get depressed because of serotonin, and there isn't much evidence about how to prevent depression in people who are more likely to get it. Several studies have looked at how to help people who are showing early signs of depression as well as how to prevent depression in the general population. Early intervention isn't as good as prevention, and even though population strategies are important, they should be paired with interventions that can be used for a long time on specific people who don't even have clinical symptoms yet. Clearly, drug treatments aren't the right way to go, and given the evidence that serotonin plays a role in both the cause and treatment of depression, non-drug methods of increasing serotonin could be tested to see if they can prevent depression.

Another reason to look for ways to increase serotonin that don't involve drugs is that people are starting to realize that happiness and well-being are important not only for the obvious reasons but also as ways to prevent disease.

On other hand, bad moods lead to bad things happening. For example, hostility is a sign of a bad mood that can lead to many different kinds of disorders. One of the main causes of death is coronary heart disease (CHD). A review of 45 studies showed that hostility is a risk factor for both CHD and death from any cause. Recent research backs this up. Patients with coronary heart disease (CHD) are more likely to die if they are hostile. This is also true for patients with coronary artery disease (CAD). Hostility can lead to less social support and social isolation, and people with CAD are more likely to die if they don't feel like they have a lot of social support. There are more effects than just CHD. For example, agreeableness, which is the opposite of hostility, was a significant factor that kept older, weaker people from dying in a study.

"Health is a state of complete physical, mental, and social well-being, not just the absence of disease or infirmity," says the WHO's (World Health Organization) constitution.

This may sound like an exaggeration, but a positive mood within the normal range is an important predictor of health and longevity. In a classic study, those in the lowest quartile for positive emotions, based on autobiographies written at an average age of 22 years, died on average 10 years before those in the highest quartile. Even when possible confounding factors were taken into account, other studies found the same strong link between feeling good and living longer. In a series of recent studies, negative emotions were linked to more mental and physical disorders that caused disability, more cases of depression, more suicides, and more death up to 20 years later. Positive feelings kept these things from happening. A recent review with meta-analyses looked at cross-sectional, longitudinal, and experimental studies and came to the conclusion that happiness is linked to and comes before many successful things. Social behavior can be affected by mood, and social support is one of the psychosocial factors linked to health and illness that has been studied the most. Low social support is linked to more stress, depression, dysthymia, and posttraumatic stress disorder, as well as more illness and death from a wide range of diseases.

Research backs up what might seem like common sense: that being happy and agreeable makes it easier to get along with other people. This, in turn, will make it possible for social support to grow, an essential facet of health.

Several studies found a link between serotonin-related measures and a normal range of mood. In one study, a lower mood was linked to a lower level of platelet serotonin receptor function, while in another, a better mood was linked to a higher level of serotonin in the blood. Two studies found that a higher amount of prolactin released by fenfluramine was linked to a better mood.

The idea that these links show a cause-and-effect relationship between serotonin function and mood within the normal range is supported by a study that showed that, compared to a placebo, tryptophan made healthy people with high trait irritability less likely to fight, more likely to be friendly, and in a better mood.

Non-drug ways to raise serotonin in the brain could help healthy people feel better and interact better with others, which would be a good thing even if nothing else was taken into account. It would also be possible to test the idea that more serotonin in the brain could help prevent the onset of mental and physical disorders. Here, we'll talk about four strategies that are worth looking into more.

Changing Your Thoughts

Using positron emission tomography, they measured how much serotonin was made in the brains of healthy people who were made to feel happy, sad, or neutral. Reports of happiness were linked to more serotonin being made in the right anterior cingulate cortex, while reports of sadness were linked to less serotonin being made.

It's not a new idea that changing your thoughts on your own or through psychotherapy can change how your brain works. Several studies have shown that the blood flow changes in these situations. Reports about specific transmitters, on the other hand, are much less common.

In a recent study, it was found that meditation caused more dopamine to be released. The study by Perreau-Linck and her team is the first to show that changing your mood on your own can affect how serotonin is made. This makes it more likely that serotonin synthesis and mood have a two-way effect on each other, with mood affecting serotonin and mood affecting serotonin. It's clear that more work needs to be done to find answers in this area.

Sunlight

Light therapy is a standard treatment for seasonal depression, but a few studies suggest that it can also help with other types of depression. It can also help women with premenstrual dysphoric disorder and depressed pregnant women feel better. There is only indirect evidence that these effects are caused by serotonin. Serotonin levels are higher in the brains of people who died in the summer than in the brains of people who died in the winter. In a study with healthy volunteers, the serotonin metabolite 5-hydroxyindoleacetic acid (5-HIAA) in the veins leaving the brain was used to measure serotonin synthesis. This study came to a similar conclusion. No matter what time of year the measurements were made, there was also a positive link between serotonin production and the amount of sunlight on the day of the measurements. The photic cycle, not the circadian rhythm, controls how much serotonin is in rats during the light part of the light-dark cycle. The fact that there is a retinography tract may help explain why retinal light exposure changes how fast neurons fire, how much c-fos is expressed, and how much serotonin is in the raphe nuclei of test animals. There is no doubt that bright light and the serotonin system interact in people as well. If the study is done in bright light (3000 lux) instead of dim light, the effect of acute tryptophan depletion on mood in healthy women is completely blocked.

A few generations ago, most people around the world worked in agriculture and spent most of the day outside. This would have meant that they were exposed to a lot of bright light even in the winter. Even on a cloudy day, there can be more than 1000 lux of light outside. This is a level of light that is almost never found indoors. In a recent study done near 45° N, people who worked at least 30 hours a week, including weekends, were exposed to light brighter than 1000 lux for about 30 minutes a day in the winter and only 90 minutes a day in the summer. This group probably saw a lot less bright light during the summer than our farming ancestors did during the winter.

On the positive effects of bright light on healthy people, there is a lot of research that goes beyond the scope of this article. Seasonal affective disorder can be treated with lamps that give off more lux than normal indoor lighting. These lamps are easy to find, but some people may find it hard to work them into their daily routines.

But there are other plans, both personal and institutional, that can be used. "Light cafes," which started in Scandinavia, are now in the UK, and an

Austrian village that doesn't get any sunlight in the winter because it's surrounded by mountains is building a series of giant mirrors to reflect sunlight into the valley. Architects are becoming more aware of the need for buildings to make better use of natural light. Working inside doesn't have to mean that you don't get enough bright light.

Exercise

Exercise is a third way that may help raise serotonin in the brain. After a thorough look at the link between exercise and mood, it was clear that exercise has antidepressant and anxiety-reducing effects. In the UK, the National Institute for Health and Clinical Excellence, which works for the National Health Service and makes treatment recommendations based on the best evidence available, has put out a guide on how to treat depression. The guide suggests that people with mild clinical depression should be treated with different methods, like exercise, instead of antidepressants, because taking antidepressants isn't worth the risk for people with mild depression. Exercise makes people feel better, both in and out of the hospital. The effect is most consistent when people who work out regularly do aerobic exercise at a level they are used to. Some people still don't believe that exercise can help with depression, so the National Institute of Mental Health in the United States is funding a clinical trial to find out. This trial will look at the antidepressant effect of exercise and try to fix problems with internal and external validity that have limited previous research.

Several types of research show that exercise makes the serotonin in the brain work better. Post and his colleagues looked at biogenic amine metabolites in the cerebrospinal fluid (CSF) of depressed people before and after they got more active to mimic mania. Physical activity increased 5-HIAA, but it is not clear if this was because serotonin was used up faster or because CSF from higher regions, which has more 5-HIAA, was mixed with CSF from the lower back (or to a combination of both mechanisms). Still, this finding led to a lot of research on the effects of exercise on animals.

Chaouloff and his colleagues found that exercise raised the levels of tryptophan and 5-HIAA in the ventricles of rats. Recent studies that used intracerebral dialysis have shown that exercise raises the levels of extracellular serotonin and 5-HIAA in the hippocampus, cortex, and other parts of the brain. This effect may happen through two different ways. Jacobs and Fornal looked at the research and found that motor activity makes serotonin neurons fire more often, which causes more serotonin to be released and made.

The most research on how exercise affects the amount of tryptophan available to the brain in humans is based on the idea that fatigue during exercise is linked to more tryptophan and serotonin being made in the brain. A lot of evidence shows that exercise, especially exercise that makes you tired, raises the level of plasma tryptophan and lowers the level of plasma branched chain amino acids (BCAAs), which are leucine, isoleucine, and valine. The BCAAs stop the brain from getting tryptophan. Because of the increase in plasma tryptophan and decrease in BCAA, there is a substantial increase in tryptophan availability to the brain.

Tryptophan works well as a mild sedative, which led to the idea that it might be involved in fatigue. Also, exercise causes the ratio of tryptophan to BCAAs in the blood to rise before fatigue sets in. The results of these studies show that a rise in the availability of precursors should increase serotonin synthesis in humans during and after exercise.

As with exposure to bright light, people's level of vigorous physical activity has changed a lot since they were hunters and gatherers or mostly worked in agriculture.

The decline in vigorous physical exercise and, in particular, effort-based rewards may contribute to the high rate of depression in today's society. The way exercise affects serotonin suggests that the exercise itself may be more important than the rewards it brings. If trials to see if exercise can prevent depression work, depression prevention can be added to the many other benefits of exercise.

Diet

Diet is the fourth thing that helps raise serotonin in the brain. But there is some disagreement about whether tryptophan should be thought of more as a drug or as a food. In the US, it is considered a food ingredient, but in Canada and some European countries, it is considered a drug. It makes sense to treat tryptophan like a drug because, first, purified tryptophan is rarely needed for dietary reasons, and second, purified tryptophan and foods with tryptophan have different effects on serotonin in the brain.

Pure tryptophan increases serotonin in the brain, but foods that contain tryptophan do not. This is because tryptophan is moved into the brain by a system that moves all large neutral amino acids, and tryptophan is the amino acid in protein that is found in the least amount. There is competition between the different amino acids for the transport system. This means that after eating a meal with protein, the rise in plasma levels of the other large neutral amino acids will stop the rise in plasma tryptophan from increasing brain tryptophan. The popular belief that a high-protein food like turkey will increase tryptophan and serotonin in the brain is not true (turkey does not make you sleepy, y'all. Feasting might.) The Internet is also full of the idea that bananas make you feel better because they have serotonin in them. Even though bananas do have serotonin, it doesn't get into the brain because of the BBB (Blood Brain Barrier)

Pellagra is a disease caused by not getting enough niacin. This is usually caused by being poor and eating a lot of corn (maize), which is low in niacin and its precursor tryptophan. Alkali was used by cultures in the Americas that grew and processed a lot of corn (e.g., boiling the corn in lime when making tortillas). This made the corn more nutritious by making it easier for the body to absorb niacin and tryptophan. This helped prevent pellagra.

Europeans took corn all over the world, but they didn't take the traditional alkali-processing methods with them. This led to outbreaks of pellagra in the past. In the 1980s, it was shown that breeding corn with more tryptophan could prevent pellagra, and it's likely that this also raised serotonin levels in the brain.

Morris and Sands argue in a recent issue of Nature Biotechnology that plant breeders should focus more on nutrition than on yield. They ask, "Could eating foods that are high in tryptophan help reduce the number of people who are depressed and violent?"

Cross-country studies have found a link between eating corn and the number of homicides and a link between eating tryptophan and the number of suicides. Even though the idea behind these studies is interesting, it is impossible to say for sure what caused what because of all the possible confounds. Still, the idea that increasing the amount of tryptophan in a population's diet compared to the amount of other amino acids in a population's diet could improve mental health is an interesting one that should be looked into further.

Pharmacological strategies aren't the only ones worth looking into when trying to figure out how to make serotonin work better in the brain. More research needs to be done on how non-drug interventions affect serotonin in the brain and how more serotonin might affect mood and behavior. Research on drugs that change serotonin is much more expensive and time-consuming than research on non-drug methods.

Socializing

People have lived in communities with lots of other people for thousands of years. And in the age of instant messaging, Uber and even Tinder, we're used to being able to see and interact with people whenever we like.

An article in The Economist talked about how being alone for a long time can cause anxiety and depression, among other mental health problems. Social isolation has also been linked to other health problems, such as cardiovascular disease, and even results in increased mortality rates.

It is very hard to study the neurobiological processes that cause changes in behavior or mood from inside a person's home. Everyone's situation is different, which makes things even more complicated. You might be self-isolating with family or all by yourself, and these small differences can make it hard to apply results to larger groups. Not to mention that we all have different ways of responding to social interactions.

So, lab animals are the best way to study how being alone affects the brain because they can be put in controlled situations. One study set out to find out how being alone affects male and female mice in a study that came out at just the right time (February).

Mice were put in their own cages when they were 3 weeks old, and they were on their own for at least 7 weeks before any tests were done. The researchers then conducted a battery of behavioral tests designed to assess the anxiety- and depression-like behaviors of the mice. Compared to mice that lived with other mice, male mice that lived alone all the time gave up on a swimming task to escape faster, which shows a lack of motivation and helplessness. They also took longer to eat in a new situation, which shows a loss of appetite. In the same way, these mice didn't like sugary water as much as the mice that lived in groups did. Based on these results, it seems that male mice that have been isolated have a more "depressed" phenotype than mice that have not been isolated.

But the opposite was true for the female mice. The housing conditions had no effect on how much the female mice tried to escape when swimming, but they ate faster when they were alone and in a new situation. Typically, this would be interpreted as an anti-depressant phenotype, but given the stress caused by single-housing, it is likely that the female mice are simply responding differently to the male mice due to neurological interactions with sex steroids, such as oestrogen and progesterone, that can alter emotional behaviours.

Interestingly, social isolation didn't seem to change how the mice responded to traditional tests of anxiety. This was confirmed when the results of all the tests were put together for a more general "emotionality" test.

While social isolation had a strong effect on behaviors that are similar to depression, it had no effect on either male or female mice's anxiety.

The researchers also wanted to find out how social isolation changed the way emotional behavior is controlled by neuronal circuits. Neurons in a part of the brain called the dorsal raphe nucleus were recorded from slices of the brains of mice that had always lived alone. This is where the neurotransmitter serotonin is made.

Like the experiments on how mice act, the neurons of male and female mice also responded in different ways. Following chronic social isolation, the neurons of male mice were less excitable, firing less than neurons from the group-housed males. On the other hand, female neurons became more excited. Even though we can't say for sure from these experiments that the differences in how males and females behave are caused by changes in serotonin neuronal activity, they do show that being alone for a long time can have a big effect on how the brain works, which correlates with how mice behave in tests.

But one important thing to note about this work is the age at which the mice started to live alone. At 3 weeks old, mice are weaned from their mothers but were still very young, not becoming sexually mature for another two to three weeks. This is the equivalent of isolating a human from their teenage years to early adulthood.

Although this is anthropomorphising the experience of the mice, there are key neurobiological developments that occur in this juvenile period that could interact with isolation to change the behavior of the mice in adulthood. Similarly, pharmacological manipulation of the serotonin system with a class of antidepressants called SSRIs (selective serotonin reuptake inhibitors, such as Paxil and Prozac) during adolescence can increase the risk of anxiety and depression in adulthood, both in humans and mice. Therefore, it would prove pertinent to compare how mice respond when isolated for the same length of time but from adulthood onwards, with normal interactions during development. Still, it's very important to know how isolation affects the developing brain, especially since so many young people are out of school and have a lot fewer friends than they used to.

So, what insight can this study in mice give to our current situation? Well, it's clear that being alone can have big effects on both the way our brains work and how we feel. But importantly it demonstrates how differently males and females respond to this stress.

Animal behavior experiments rarely look at how females act, so not much is known about why these differences happen. This paper shows how important it is to study both sexes in all behavior experiments, even with patients.

More generally, if the effects of chronic isolation in mice can be extrapolated to humans, it means that people who live alone could have serious mental health problems in the coming months. We need to be willing to put money into mental health services and research to help people get better. But most importantly, we need to do everything we can to stay in touch and help others with a simple, friendly conversation or invitation to do something. Kindness has the power to heal.

Chapter 6: Optimism

What is going on in the brain when one produces positive or negative thoughts?

Every thought releases some type of chemical. When positive thoughts are generated, when you're feeling happy, or optimistic, cortisol decreases and the brain produces serotonin, creating a feeling of well-being. When serotonin levels are normal, one feels happy, calmer, less anxious, more focused and more emotionally stable. Dopamine is also a neurotransmitter that helps control the brain's reward system and pleasure center.

Positive Thinking

Daniel Goleman, author of "Focus: The Hidden Driver of Excellence," states that the brain has heightened prefrontal activity and positivity resulting in enhanced mental functions such as creative thinking, cognitive flexibility, and even faster processing. Positive emotions actually widen our attention span, and it also changes our perception and focus on more of the "we" instead of the "me."

Taking a look at the prefrontal cortex, when happy thoughts occur, there is brain growth through the reinforcement and generation of new synapses. The prefrontal cortex is where all brain functions conjugate and then are disbursed to various parts of the brain or transmitted to other parts of the body. The prefrontal cortex is the switching station that regulates the signals from the neurons as well as what allows you to reflect and think about what you are doing at the time. It allows you to control your emotions through your limbic brain. Since it allows you to focus, it also gives you time for metacognition (being aware of one's own thought processes).

Negative Thinking

When you're having negative thoughts, the brain actually draws precious metabolic energy away from the prefrontal cortex. With these negative thoughts, the brain can't perform at high or even normal capacity. When stressed or scared, it's difficult to take in and process new material, let alone think creatively. Stress can alter plasticity in the nervous system, particularly in the limbic system.

Single photon emission computed tomography (SPECT) brain imaging studies have shown that negative thoughts also reduce activity in the cerebellum, which controls coordination, balance, working relationships with others as well as speed of thought.

Emotional pain is hardwired into the brain in a way that physical pain is not. Hence, we can re-live it over and over in our minds. The emotional tone of a boss delivering criticism to the employee will have a greater effect on the individual than the actual statements themselves. Likewise, the emotional tone of the teacher delivering feedback to a student will have more of an impact than the actual feedback itself.

The frontal lobe, particularly the prefrontal cortex, decides the amount of attention to pay to something based on its importance and how you feel about it. The more you focus on negativity, the more synapses and neurons your brain will create – supporting your negative thought process. Negative thoughts slow down the brain's ability to function and it impedes cognition.

Glass Half-full or Half-empty?

Behavioral scientists have also observed some interesting differences between optimists and pessimists. Besides the fact that optimists are more successful in life, they also tend to have better physical health. Being optimistic involves highly desirable cognitive, emotional, and motivational components.

Negative Thoughts

- Slow down brain coordination
- Make it difficult to process thoughts ... or find solutions
- Hinders creative ability
- Decreases activity in the cerebellum
- Impacts the left temporal lobe (fear factor), affecting mood, memory and impulse control

Positive Thoughts

- Synapses (areas connecting neurons) increase dynamically
- Increases mental productivity by improving cognition
- Intensifies ability to pay attention, to focus
- Improves ability to think and analyze incoming data
- Improves ability to solve problems quicker
- Enhances creativity

So, to get better at learning — to improve our thinking – we need to keep our brains happy.

Chapter 7: Melatonin

Melatonin (a hormone) is something that acts like a neurotransmitter. It is an important part of how our circadian rhythm, or body clock, works. Our circadian rhythm controls hormone release, body temperature, and how we sleep.

In terms of hormones, serotonin and melatonin are almost like day and night. Even though they do different jobs, they must work together to keep the body in balance.

Serotonin can be described as our body's natural happiness drug. It's a "feel-good" hormone that makes us happier and more relaxed and gives us more energy all around. This energy is especially important because we all need it to wake up in the morning and get rid of the tiredness that would keep us in bed otherwise.

Melatonin is on the other end of the scale. Melatonin is the "darkness hormone," which isn't as scary as it sounds. The name comes from the fact that the pineal gland in the brain makes melatonin when it is dark. Any sleep expert will tell you that turning off the lights and using black-out blinds or an eye mask in the bedroom is a great way to start the sleep cycle. This is because when the light changes, the eye sends a message to the brain saying that it should make more melatonin. Melatonin slows down the body, making it more tired and ready for sleep.

Without melatonin, it would be impossible to sleep in a calm, restful way, and the body wouldn't be able to do the healing it usually does while you're asleep.

Your body makes more melatonin when it's dark, but it makes more serotonin when it's sunny or bright. In short, melatonin helps you fall asleep, and serotonin helps you feel awake when you wake up the next day.

If you don't have enough melatonin, you might have trouble sleeping or even insomnia. If you don't have enough serotonin, you might feel sad and tired.

How can melatonin and serotonin be used to help you sleep well?

The easiest way to use these hormones to get a good night's sleep is to increase your melatonin levels at night and your serotonin levels in the morning.

It's not as hard as you may think. To get more melatonin at night, just turn down the lights in the evening and stay away from bright screens for a while before bed. Meditation is also thought to be a good way to help you wind down before bed.

The next day, everything is about letting light in. Open the curtains and let in as much sunlight as you can to raise your serotonin level. Even better, go outside and breathe some fresh air.

You can also get more melatonin and serotonin from the food you eat. Cherries have a lot of melatonin in them, and bananas, oatmeal, and milk help the body make more of it.

Melatonin can also be bought as a supplement in the United States. Melatonin supplements come in many forms, such as pills, liquids, and patches. Most people only take melatonin supplements short-term, but studies have been done that have lasted up to two years, wherein the participants took melatonin daily and no adverse effects were observed.

Some people, like shift workers or those with delayed sleep-wake phase disorder, can use melatonin to reset their internal body clocks and sleep better. Melatonin is often called the "sleep hormone," but it may have other important roles besides controlling sleep. For example, it might help calm your nerves before surgery.

Melatonin is generally well tolerated and doesn't cause side effects, so it can be a safe short-term solution for sleep problems. Most prescription sleep aids have this in common. Studies have shown that it can help you fall asleep seven minutes faster, add eight minutes to your total sleep time, and improve the quality of your sleep as a whole.

Because the U.S. Food and Drug Administration considers it a dietary supplement, there are no official guidelines for melatonin dosage in the United States. How much melatonin is safe to take depends on your age, body weight, and how sensitive you are to it.

Melatonin Dosage for Adults

There is no official recommended amount of melatonin for

adults, but a range of 1 mg to 5 mg has been used.

Melatonin for women who are pregnant or who are nursing

Women who are pregnant or who are nursing should not take melatonin without first talking to their doctor. There hasn't been enough research into whether or not melatonin is safe for this group.

Melatonin Dosage for Older Adults

As a person gets older, their melatonin levels naturally go down. As a result, older adults may have an increased sensitivity to melatonin. In a meta-analysis of 16 studies, older adults aged 55 to 77 were given melatonin doses between 0.1 milligrams and 50 milligrams per kilogram. In all of the studies, the melatonin levels of older adults were higher and stayed higher for longer than those of younger adults. This made older adults feel sleepier during the day. The stronger these effects were, the more melatonin the person had taken.

So, researchers say that older people should start with the smallest amount of melatonin possible. Smaller doses might help older people sleep better without messing up their circadian rhythms or making them sleepy for a long time.

The American Academy of Sleep Medicine says that people with dementia should not take melatonin.

Melatonin Dosage for Children

Most children seem to be able to handle small doses of melatonin for short periods of time, but parents should talk to their child's doctor before giving them melatonin. The right dose for a child depends on what is making them have trouble sleeping. Insomnia in children is usually treated with doses of 1 to 2 milligrams.

When children take melatonin, side effects may include:

- Agitation
- Bedwetting
- Dizziness
- Drowsiness
- Headaches

Melatonin may be given to children with sleep problems, such as insomnia, autism spectrum disorder, or attention-deficit hyperactivity disorder, by their doctors. Several studies have shown that giving children with these conditions melatonin supplements can make them sleep 25 to 48 minutes longer on average.

But there haven't been enough studies of melatonin in children for experts to decide on an official recommended dose or any possible long-term safety risks. Since melatonin is a hormone, taking extra melatonin might affect other parts of a child's hormone development, but more research is needed. Experts say that if your child is having trouble sleeping, you should talk to your doctor before giving them melatonin. Research shows that in half of the situations where melatonin was used to treat pediatric insomnia, better sleep habits were just as effective at relieving the child's sleep problems.

What dosage of Melatonin should I take?

It is best to start with the smallest amount of melatonin that is recommended for your age. From there, you can slowly increase your dose until you find one that helps you fall asleep without giving you any side effects. Most of the time, 1 to 5 milligrams of melatonin is a safe starting dose for adults. For older adults, doses of less than 1 milligram may work. Melatonin shouldn't be given to kids unless a doctor says so.

Melatonin that you can buy over-the-counter may come in standard amounts like 1, 3, or 5 milligrams. To make a smaller starting dose, you can use a pill cutter to cut the tablets in half or in quarters. Dosages of 0.3 and 0.1 can be purchased on Amazon and tend to cost much less.

Melatonin: When to Talk to Your Doctor

Before taking any over-the-counter sleep aid, including melatonin, it's always a good idea to talk to your doctor first. They know your health history and can give you the best advice about how much melatonin you should take. They will also know if melatonin could have a bad effect on any other medicines you are taking.

When you take melatonin, you may be more likely to have side effects if you have certain health conditions or are taking certain medicines. Before taking melatonin, you should talk to your doctor if you take any of the following drugs:

- Oral contraceptives
- Immunosuppressants or corticosteroids
- Blood pressure-lowering medicines
- Warfarin or other blood thinning medicines

Also, the following groups of people may be more sensitive to melatonin and shouldn't take it until they've talked to their doctor:

- Children
- Those who have dementia
- People with depression
- People who have seizures
- Women who are pregnant or who are nursing
- Shift workers

Melatonin's possible benefits and uses are still being studied, and its long-term effects are still not clear.

When used for a short time, melatonin helps many people with sleep problems in small ways. For some people, it may have side effects or have no effect at all on sleep.

If you try melatonin and it doesn't help you sleep, you might want to talk to a doctor. They can also suggest other ways to help you sleep better, like better sleep hygiene, changes to your diet and exercise routine, or cognitive-behavioral therapy for insomnia. They can also look into other things that might be making it hard for you to sleep.

What makes melatonin directly relevant to serotonin is that serotonin converts into melatonin. If your serotonin levels are low, your melatonin levels may also be low as a result. Melatonin also can convert back into serotonin. Therefore, if your melatonin levels are low, your serotonin levels may be low as a result.

Chapter 8: 5-HTP

5-HTP, a supplement, is 5-hydroxytryptophan. It comes from the seed of the Griffonia Simplicifolia plant, and it is a building block for serotonin.

To get the benefits of 5-HTP, you should take 300–500 mg of it every day.

Antidepressants SHOULD NOT be taken with 5-HTP. Serotonin syndrome may result which, at the very least will cause tremendous suffering, and at the worst, cause death, though it rarely gets to that point.

WHAT IS 5-HTP?

5-HTP is made when your brain turns the amino acid L-Tryptophan into serotonin.

It is used to treat things like depression, insomnia, and anxiety, among other things. 5-HTP is an easy and effective way to boost serotonin in the brain.

5-HTP BENEFITS

Some of the benefits of 5-HTP are:

- Improves sleep
- Combats night terrors
- Could be good for depression
- Lessens stress and worry

Let's look at the research behind these claims.

Sleep

We already know that serotonin is made from 5-HTP in the body. Even better is that this serotonin can be turned into melatonin. We already know that melatonin can help you fall asleep faster and have a better night's sleep.

But there's one catch with 5-HTP and how well you sleep. That is, it only works when it is combined with GABA (gamma-aminobutyric acid).

One example is a study done by Shell et al. in 2010. This study was random, double-blind, and controlled by a placebo. It was real, in other words. Researchers chose 18 people with sleep problems at random and put them in either a group that got 5-HTP and GABA or a group that got only 5-HTP.

They measured variables such as sleep quality via a visual scale, sleep latency and duration using daily questionnaires, and autonomic nervous system function by measuring heart rate variability.

In the treatment group, it took 19 minutes less time to fall asleep, but there was no change in the placebo group. In the treatment group, the amount of time spent sleeping went up by about 2 hours. In the placebo group, the amount of time spent sleeping went up by 30 minutes.

Ease of falling asleep, awakenings, and morning grogginess

improved in the treatment group but not the placebo group.

In the treatment group, the parasympathetic system got better, but not in the placebo group.

Overall, people who took the 5-HTP/GABA supplement fell asleep faster, stayed asleep longer, had better quality sleep, and fell asleep faster than people who took a placebo.

Nightmares

The good news is that 5-HTP may help stop scary dreams.

Bruni et al. did a study in 2004 in which 45 people who had had night terrors in the past were given either 5-HTP or a placebo every night for 20 days. Researchers found that people who took 5-HTP had a lot fewer night terrors than those who took a placebo during the 20 days and for the next 6 months.

Depression

We've already talked about how 5-HTP can raise the amount of serotonin in the brain. This is the main way that people think 5-HTP can help with depression. But this claim needs more solid evidence to fully back it up.

When people with depression take 5-HTP, their symptoms get better, but most of the studies aren't controlled by a placebo or combine 5-HTP with other chemicals, which makes the results harder to understand.

In one such study, it was found that the combination of 5-HTP and carbidopa helped 43 out of 99 clinically depressed people get better from their treatment. The daily dose was 50–600 mg.

Stress

Breaking up with a spouse or boyfriend/girlfriend is one of the most stressful things that can happen. Let science figure out if 5-HTP can make the stress of being dumped less painful.

In 2010, Emanuele et al. did a study with 15 healthy people (11 women and 4 men) who had recently broken up with someone and were very upset about it. Researchers had the people take 60mg of 5-HTP every day for 6 weeks. They were checked at the start, after 3 weeks, and at the end of the 6 week period. Using questionnaires and measuring serotonin levels, they found that stress scores were much lower than at the start and that platelet serotonin levels were higher.

5-HTP DOSE

Most studies have used a daily dose of 300–500mg to get the above benefits. This dose can be taken all at once or split into two doses to be taken at different times of the day.

The 5-HTP should be standardized to 98% and come from the Griffonia Simplicifolia plant. This is a very important part of the dosage.

There is some evidence that 5-HTP can make you feel less hungry, which can help you lose weight. If you want to do this with 5-HTP, you should take it with food.

How Often to Take It

As a general rule, you should take 5-HTP every day. Even though it helps right away, research shows that it works better when taken for 20 days or more. You can it 20 to 30 minutes before bed to help you sleep, with breakfast first thing in the morning if you want to reduce stress and worry or with a meal if you want to lose weight.

How Long Before it Works?

In as little as 30–45 minutes, 5-HTP can start to work to raise serotonin levels in the brain.

Side-Effects

Overall, only a small number of people have side effects from taking 5-HTP. Some of these side effects can be:

- Nausea
- Muscle tenderness

Who Can't Take 5-HTP?

Taking 5-HTP with other drugs or supplements that increase serotonin is dangerous.

Where Can I Get 5-HTP?

5-HTP can be bought online or at any drugstore or health food store.

Chapter 9: Serotonin Syndrome

Too much serotonin in your body can cause serotonin syndrome, which is a drug reaction that could kill you. Serotonin is a chemical that nerve cells in your brain and other parts of your body make.

Most people can take serotonin-affecting (serotonergic) drugs safely if they are prescribed at the right dose and taken as directed by their doctor. Most of the time, serotonin syndrome happens when you take a new drug or a higher dose of a drug that makes your body make more serotonin. Serotonin syndrome symptoms can happen if your body doesn't handle serotonin the same way or if it can't handle a lot of serotonin.

Serotonin syndrome can cause mild symptoms (like diarrhea or nausea) or severe symptoms. Severe serotonin syndrome can sometimes be fatal if it is not caught and treated quickly.

Healthcare providers first recognized serotonin syndrome in the 1960s, after the approval of the first antidepressant medications. Today, there are more medicines that affect serotonin. This has led to a growing number of cases of serotonin syndrome.

Who gets serotonin syndrome?

Serotonin syndrome could happen to anyone who takes certain prescription drugs, over-the-counter drugs, herbal or dietary supplements, or illegal drugs that change the amount of serotonin in the body. It can happen to anyone at any time.

Signs and Symptoms

The symptoms of serotonin syndrome vary from person to person, as does how bad they are. They can be mild, serious, or even kill you.

If you are taking a drug that affects serotonin and have any of the following symptoms, call your doctor or go to an urgent care or emergency room right away.

Mild symptoms:

- Nervousness
- Nausea
- Vomiting
- Diarrhea
- Dilated pupils
- Tremor
- Moderate illness
- Unease and agitation
- Muscle twitching
- Muscle spasms
- Muscle rigidity
- Involuntary muscle contractions
- Getting hot and cold
- Abnormal (side-to-side) eye movements

Severe symptoms

- Confusion
- Disorientation
- Delirium
- Fast heartbeat

- High blood-pressure
- High body temperature (greater than 101.3 Fahrenheit [38.5 Celsius]).
- Seizures
- Irregular heartbeat
- Fainting

How soon do the signs and symptoms of serotonin syndrome show up?

Symptoms usually start within a few hours of taking a new drug that affects serotonin levels or increasing the dose of a drug you are already taking. Almost everyone will start to feel sick within 24 hours of taking a serotonin-boosting drug or product for the first time, adding it to their routine, or increasing the amount they take.

How does serotonin syndrome happen?

Serotonin syndrome is when the amount of serotonin in your body goes up. This rise in serotonin can occur if:

- Take more than one medication that affects serotonin levels.
- Just started taking a new drug or upped the dose of a drug that is known to raise serotonin levels.
- Take too much of a drug that affects serotonin, either by accident or on purpose.
- Use illegal drugs, herbal products, or over-the-counter medicines that change the amount of serotonin in your body.

What drugs and other things can change serotonin levels and cause serotonin syndrome?

Antidepressants

Most of the time, people take antidepressants to change their serotonin levels. When they are the cause of serotonin syndrome, they are often used with other serotonin-related drugs that treat other conditions, like triptans for migraines or opioids for pain.

Some types of antidepressants and medications that can raise serotonin levels are:

- Selective serotonin reuptake inhibitors (SSRIs): This class includes fluoxetine (Prozac®), citalopram (Celexa®), sertraline

(Zoloft®), paroxetine (Paxil®) and escitalopram (Lexapro®). This type of antidepressant is the most likely to cause serotonin syndrome because it is used so often.

- Serotonin-norepinephrine reuptake inhibitors (SNRIs): This group includes duloxetine (Cymbalta®), venlafaxine (Effexor®), desvenlafaxine (Pristiq), levomilnacipran (Fetzima®), and milnacipran (Savella).
- Tricyclic antidepressants include amitriptyline (Elavil®), clomipramine (Anafranil®), nortriptyline (Pamelor®), desipramine (Norpramin®), doxepin (Sinequan®), imipramine (Tofranil®), and

trimipramine
(Surmontil®).

- Ohenelzine (Nardil®),
  selegiline (Emsam®), and
  tranylcypromine
  (Parnate®).
- Serotonin modulators
  like nefazodone and
  trazodone (Desyrel®)
- Norepinephrine reuptake
  inhibitor: This class
  includes bupropion
  (Wellbutrin®).

Other drugs can also change the amount of serotonin in your body, especially when they are taken with other drugs that change serotonin. These medicines are used to:

- Drugs used to treat
  severe pain, such as
  Morphine
- Cough and cold
  medicines sold over-the-
  counter (OTC) that
  contain
  dextromethorphan

- HIV/AIDS: Ritonavir (Norvir®).
- Antibiotic: Linezolid (Zyvox®).
- Anti-nausea medications: Metoclopramide (Reglan®), granisetron (Sustol®), droperidol (Inapsine®) and ondansetron (Zofran®).
- Lithium (Lithobid®) is a mood stabilizer.

Other things

Other things that affect serotonin levels and could cause serotonin syndrome are:

- Herbal supplements: Ginseng, St. John's wort, Syrian rue, and nutmeg are some examples.
- Illegal drugs: Ecstasy, LSD, cocaine, amphetamines, and methamphetamines
- Tryptophan supplements

There is still a lot that doctors don't know about serotonin syndrome. If you are worried about how the medicines you take might affect serotonin, talk to your doctor or a pharmacist in your area.

Diagnosis and Tests

How do doctors find out if someone has serotonin syndrome?

There are no tests that can tell if someone has serotonin symptoms. Your doctor usually makes the diagnosis based on the results of your physical exam, a review of your symptoms, and a history of the medicines you take that affect your serotonin levels.

You can help your doctor if you tell them about everything you take, including prescription drugs, over-the-counter drugs, supplements, herbal products, and even illegal drugs. (Be honest. Don't be afraid. Your doctor is there to help you, not to judge you.)

Your doctor or nurse may tell you to:

- There are blood and urine tests to find out how much of a drug you are taking.
- There are tests to see how well your body is working.
- Tests, like a spinal tap, to look for signs of an infection.
- As needed, other tests, such as a chest X-ray or a CT scan, to rule out other diseases that could cause similar symptoms or to find any complications.

How to Treat It

Your treatment will depend on how bad your symptoms are. If your symptoms are mild, you can usually get rid of them by stopping the medicine or changing the amount you take. If your symptoms don't go away quickly, a serotonin blocker like cyproheptadine (Periactin®) may be given to you.

If your symptoms are moderate, you may be kept in the hospital for at least 24 hours to make sure they are getting better.

If your symptoms are severe, you will be put in the intensive care unit (ICU), where you can be closely monitored.

Depending on your symptoms, some possible treatments are:

- A sedative, like benzodiazepines, to help with symptoms like agitation, stiff muscles, and movements that look like seizures
- IV fluids to rehydrate you and treat your fever
- Oxygen through a mask to increase the amount of oxygen in your blood

- Heart rate and blood pressure-lowering medicines
- A breathing tube for mechanical ventilation, sedation, and paralysis of the muscles to bring down a very high fever (106 Fahrenheit [41.1 Celsius])
- Cyproheptadine, which blocks serotonin, can be used if other treatments don't work or don't work fast enough

If an antidepressant caused your serotonin syndrome, it may take a few weeks for the drug to leave your body and for your symptoms to go away completely.

Don't stop taking your medicine or change the amount you take without first talking to your doctor or nurse. But you should go to the emergency room if your symptoms are severe or if they are getting worse.

What are the problems that can come with serotonin syndrome?

If serotonin symptoms are not treated, they can lead to:

- Seizures
- Difficulty breathing
- Kidney failure
- Coma
- Death

Prevention

You should keep close track of all the medicines you take. Read all of the warnings on the package or informational sheet for your drug. They will tell you if serotonin syndrome is a possibility. Don't stop taking any medicine without first talking to your doctor or nurse. Tell all of your healthcare providers about the prescription drugs, over-the-counter drugs, herbs and supplements, and illegal drugs you take.

If you take an antidepressant (especially an SSRI or SNRI) and a triptan headache medicine at the same time, your doctor should watch you very closely. Since different subtypes of the receptor are being aimed at, the risk is thought to be low or even nonexistent. The American Migraine Foundation thinks that the combination is generally safe, and that the benefits are more important than the risks. But don't forget that you have a part to play, too. If you have any of the symptoms listed in this article, call your doctor.

By taking these steps, you and your health care team will be able to spot early signs of serotonin syndrome. If you find the problem early, you might not get worse symptoms.

Prognosis

Most people with serotonin syndrome will have all of their symptoms go away within 24 to 72 hours if they are quickly diagnosed and treated.

After you get better, your doctor or nurse can:

- Reduce the amount of the medicine that is causing the rise in serotonin to the lowest dose that works
- Don't give someone two high-dose medications that affect serotonin
- Change your medicine to one or more that doesn't affect serotonin

Selective Serotonin Reuptake Inhibitors (SSRIs)

Selective serotonin reuptake inhibitors (SSRIs) inhibit the reuptake of serotonin in the brain. Reuptake is a process where neurotransmitters in the brain are reabsorbed and deactivated or recycled for future use. When reuptake of serotonin is inhibited, more serotonin is available in the brain. This leads to an increase of serotonin levels, resulting in improved mood, decreased anxiety, and inhibition of panic.

SSRIs are considered the first-line treatment for conditions such as depression and panic disorder. SSRI medications include:

- Celexa (citalopram)
- Lexapro (escitalopram)
- Luvox (fluvoxamine)
- Paxil (paroxetine)
- Prozac (fluoxetine)
- Trintellix (vortioxetine)

- Viibryd (vilazodone)
- Zoloft (sertraline)

SSRIs are approved in the treatment of a variety of mental health conditions including generalized anxiety disorder (GAD), major depressive disorder (MDD), obsessive-compulsive disorder (OCD), post-traumatic stress disorder (PTSD), and social anxiety disorder (SAD).

SSRIs are antidepressant medications that work by blocking the reuptake of the neurotransmitter serotonin. This results in increased serotonin levels in the brain, which can improve mood and reduce anxiety.

Serotonin-Norepinephrine Reuptake Inhibitors (SNRIs)

SNRIs inhibit the reabsorption of both serotonin and norepinephrine in the brain. Norepinephrine is a neurotransmitter that influences sleep and alertness. It is believed to be correlated to the fight-or-flight stress response.

Some SNRIs include:

- Cymbalta (duloxetine)
- Effexor (venlafaxine)
- Fetzima (levomilnacipran)
- Pristiq (desvenlafaxine)
- Savella (milnacipran)

Triptans

Triptans are a class of drugs commonly used to treat migraine or cluster headaches. They act on serotonin receptors in the brain, thereby affecting serotonin levels.

Examples of triptans include:

- Amerge (naratriptan)
- Axert (almotriptan)
- Frova (frovatriptan)
- Imitrex (sumatriptan)
- Maxalt and Maxalt-MLT (rizatriptan)

- Relpax (eletriptan)
- Zomig and Zomig ZMT (zolmitriptan)

Tricyclic Antidepressants

Tricyclic antidepressants (TCAs) are named after the drugs' three-ringed molecular structure. Prior to the introduction of SSRIs in the late 1980s, TCAs were the medication of choice for the treatment of major depressive disorder, panic disorder, and other anxiety disorders. TCAs are also used to treat certain pain syndromes and nocturnal enuresis (bedwetting). It is believed that TCAs function by increasing levels of norepinephrine and serotonin in the brain.

Examples of TCAs include:

- Elavil (amitriptyline)
- Tofranil (imipramine)
- Sinequan (doxepin)
- Anafranil (clomipramine)

TCAs are used less frequently today in the treatment of depression because they tend to produce more unwanted side effects compared to SSRIs.

Monoamine Oxidase Inhibitors (MAOIs)

MAOIs are a class of antidepressants believed to increase levels of norepinephrine, serotonin, and dopamine (another neurotransmitter) in the brain. They are effective for the treatment of major depressive disorder, panic disorder, and other anxiety disorders.

Examples of MAOIs include:

- Nardil (phenelzine)
- Parnate (tranylcypromine)
- Marplan (isocarboxazid)
- Emsam (selegiline)

Because of potentially dangerous interactions with certain foods, beverages, and other drugs, particularly those that influence serotonin, MAOIs are usually not considered as a first-line treatment for depression.

Other Psychiatric Medications

There are also other psychiatric medications that can influence serotonin levels in the body:

- Buspar (buspirone): BuSpar affects the neurotransmitters serotonin and dopamine. It acts as an agonist on serotonin receptors, which means that it increases the actions of these receptors. As a result, this medication can be useful for relieving symptoms of anxiety.
- Eskalith (lithium): This medication is a mood stabilizer that is used in the treatment of bipolar disorder. It works by restoring the balance of

neurotransmitters, including serotonin.

- Desyrel (trazodone): Desyrel is an antidepressant medication that works by increasing the amount of serotonin available in the body. It also has sedative effects, which is why it is sometimes used to treat insomnia.

Analgesics (Painkillers)

A number of analgesic drugs can also affect serotonin levels in the body. These medications are often used to treat pain, but they are also sometimes misused and can lead to dependence and addiction. Some painkillers that act on serotonin include:

- Codeine
- Fentanyl
- Tramadol

Antibiotic/Antiretroviral Medications

Some antibiotics and antiretroviral medications may also affect serotonin. This can potentially lead to drug interactions when people are taking other medications such as SSRIs or MAOIs. Because of these risks, you should always tell your healthcare provider about other medications, drugs, or supplements you are currently taking.

- Zyvox (linezolid): Zyvox is an antibiotic that is sometimes prescribed to treat serious bacterial infections. In addition to inhibiting bacterial growth, this medication also affects serotonin. This affect can be more pronounced when Zyvox is combined with other serotonin medications.
- Norvir (ritonavir): Norvir is an antiviral medication

that is used to treat HIV infection. When combined with other medications, it works to slow the progress of the disease.

Herbal Drugs/Dietary Supplements

It is important to be aware that some herbal medicines and dietary supplements can have an effect on serotonin levels.

- St. John's wort (hypericum perforatum) is a type of flowering plant that is sometimes used as an herbal remedy, particularly to relieve symptoms of depression. It is also used for other conditions including anxiety, premenstrual syndrome (PMS), menopause symptoms, smoking cessation, and seasonal affective disorder. Researchers are not entirely sure of exactly how St. John's wort works to elevate mood, but it is believed to increase neurotransmitter levels in the brain, including serotonin.

- Ginseng is a root that is often used as an herbal supplement. Purported benefits include improved immunity, energy, and cognition. Ginseng acts on serotonin and other transmitters and also affects hormones, receptors, and signaling molecules. Research suggests that ginseng is associated with interactions with some psychotropic medications, including SSRI and SNRI antidepressants.

Even More Drugs That Affect Serotonin

There are also a number of other substances that can affect serotonin levels in the body:

- o Amphetamine stimulants are often prescribed to treat attention-deficit hyperactivity disorder (ADHD). These medications can also increase serotonin levels. While usually not enough to present a risk when taken as prescribed, stimulant medications such as Adderall may increase the risk of serotonin syndrome if they are misused or are combined with other serotonin medications.

- Cocaine blocks the reuptake of serotonin. This can be potentially risky if people use cocaine while they are taking antidepressants, triptans, or other medications that also increase serotonin levels.
- Lysergic acid diethylamide (LSD) is a hallucinogenic drug that affects thinking and moods. These effects are the result of the impact of the drug on serotonin. The drug binds to certain receptors in the brain and changes how the brain responds to serotonin. Combining antidepressant medications and LSD has the potential to produce unwanted effects associated with serotonin toxicity.

Chapter 11: Nature and Nurture

Monoamines, and serotonin in particular, have been linked to a number of mental health problems, including depression, anxiety, antisocial behavior, and addiction. Many studies have shown that the genes that code for monoamine oxidase A (MAOA) and the serotonin transporter (5HTT) can affect how likely someone is to get these conditions.

Serotonin has been shown to affect the growth of terminals from serotonergic neurons both directly and indirectly through an auto-regulatory feedback loop. The negative feedback loop seems to depend on the 5HT1A receptor, which is expressed early in development on serotonergic neurons and in specific parts of the limbic circuitry. This means that having too much serotonin while the brain is still growing could affect not only the neurocircuitry but also the size and capacity of the serotonergic system itself. This could help explain in part the strange link between genetic variants linked to higher levels of available serotonin (low-functioning alleles of MAOA and 5HTT) and the link between lower levels of serotonin in the brain and its metabolite 5HIAA in cerebrospinal fluid and certain behavioral traits and mental disorders.

Or, to put it another way, the low-functioning variants of MAOA and 5HTT could be linked to a higher risk of psychiatric disorders due to higher levels of serotonin during CNS development, which changes the way neurocircuits that are important for processing emotions work while also stopping the serotonergic system from growing.

Neurons in parts of the brain that control how we feel set the stage for how we react to things outside of ourselves. We've already talked about how serotonin could affect some of these neurocircuits, which seems to have effects on shaping different kinds of behavior. From this, it follows that genetic differences that lead to changes in serotonergic neurotransmission will affect how people understand and react to environmental cues, like stressful or scary ones.

But in this way, processing emotions is not a one-way street that can be explained by the shape and activity of these neuronal circuits alone.

In a well-known study by Caspi et al., it was shown that environmental stress and genetic factors worked together to change the phenotype. In a sample of male teens, those who carried the low-functioning version of the MAOA-LPR gene and had also been abused as children were more likely to act in an antisocial way.

Similar results have been seen in depression, where people with a low-functioning version of 5HTTLPR were more likely to get depressed when stressful things happened in their lives.

Based on these results, it seems that the effect of a genetic factor on behavior is affected by the environment. In multiple studies of how genes interact with the environment, it has been found that the effects of different socio-environmental factors, along with the genotypes of the MAOA-LPR and 5HTTLPR, on behavioral outcomes are also different for men and women.

A study by Nilsson et al. confirmed that males who were exposed to a bad psychosocial environment showed more antisocial behavior. This was especially true for people who carried the low-functioning version of the MAOA-LPR gene.

In a follow-up study, it was found that this genetic variation was linked to less antisocial behavior among female. Researchers have also found that genetic differences in the MAOA-LPR between men and women have opposite effects on alcohol-related problems caused by a bad psychosocial environment.

Also, the 5HTTLPR and depressive symptoms show a similar pattern of being different for men and women. Possible reasons why these responses are different for men and women could be found in a number of different ways and at different stages of development.

In the past, gonadal hormones were seen as the main cause of sexually dimorphic traits. However, over time, a more complex pattern of interactions between hormones, sex-linked gene expression, and environmental factors through epigenetic processes has been discovered.

There is a clear difference between the sexes in the number of neuropsychiatric disorders. For example, women are more likely to have major depressive disorder, generalized anxiety disorder, and post-traumatic stress disorder, while men are more likely to have antisocial personality disorder, ADHD, and alcohol and drug dependence.

Recent research seems to point to a growing consensus that the male and female brains are different in many ways, both in how they look and how they work. These differences between men and women could mean that the causes and progression of neuropsychiatric disorders could be related to changes in the CNS in different ways.

Also, different genetic variants that cause different levels of serotonin in the central nervous system (CNS) during brain development have been shown to control how people react to stressful events in their early lives. However, unpleasant stimuli seem to affect brain development after birth regardless of genetic background.

Spinelli et al. did a study on rhesus macaques that were either raised by their mother or by other monkeys. They found that stress in early life caused by peer-rearing led to stable changes in brain regions that have been linked to neuropsychiatric disorders in humans. Other studies with animal models have shown that early life stress can affect neurotrophic factors like brain-derived neurotrophic factor (BDNF) and nerve growth factor (NGF), which are known to be important for the development of neurocircuits involved in processing emotions.

Stress-related changes to BDNF during postnatal brain development are especially interesting because BDNF seems to interact functionally with serotonin in brain morphogenesis, which is supported by a human fMRI study that showed that epistasis between BDNF and 5HTT affects both volume and functional connectivity within parts of the limbic circuitry.

Studies with animal models have also shown that stress in early life can affect serotonergic neurotransmission by changing the way 5HTT and serotonin receptors are expressed and by reducing the number of serotonin neuronal axons in certain parts of the brain.

Chapter 12: Chemical Imbalances?

The chemical imbalance theory of depression is well and truly dead. A paper by Joanna Moncrieff and colleagues, longtime critics of the effectiveness of antidepressants, has caused a big splash. The paper provides a summary of other summaries that confirm there is no evidence to support the idea that depression is caused by disturbance of the brain's serotonin system.

But the death of the chemical imbalance theory has no bearing on whether antidepressants that affect the serotonin system are effective. These medications weren't developed on this premise. In fact. quite the opposite is true – the chemical imbalance theory was based on an emerging understanding of how antidepressants were shown to work.

How did the "chemical imbalance" theory start?

The first two antidepressant medications, both discovered in the 1950s, were observed to have positive effects on mood as side-effects of their hoped-for functions. Iproniazid was developed as a treatment for tubercolosis and imipramine as an antihistamine.

We know now that ipronizaid is a monoamine oxidase inhibitor – it stops the enzyme that breaks down serotonin and similar brain chemicals. But we didn't know this when its antidepressant effects were first observed in 1952.

Imipramine is a tricyclic antidepressant, and, among other effects, it blocks the reuptake of serotonin after it has been secreted, also allowing more to stay in the brain.

A simple hypothesis then presented itself: if both classes of antidepressants were shown to increase brain levels of serotonin, then depression must be caused by low levels of serotonin. Researchers set out to demonstrate this in patients with depression, showing that serotonin and its metabolites and precursors were lower in the blood, in the cerebrospinal fluid, and so on.

But these studies suffered from what we now know plagued many studies of their era, leading to the so-called "replication crisis." Studies used small sample sizes, selectively reported their results and, if they failed to demonstrate the hypothesis, were often not reported at all. In short, the findings were unreliable, and since then larger studies and meta-analyses (which summarized the many smaller studies) made it clear the hypothesis wasn't supported.

What's the link between the theory and antidepressants?

In the meantime, pharmaceutical companies spotted a clear line to communicate the effectiveness of their medications. Depression was caused by a "chemical imbalance" that could be corrected by antidepressants. This coincided with the development of a new class of antidepressants, the selective serotonin reuptake inhibitors, which, as their name suggests, were more selective than the tricyclic antidepressants in targeting serotonin reuptake as their mechanism of action.

There were few psychiatrists who knew enough about how the brain works to know that the chemical imbalance theory was false. It didn't make sense with how they knew SSRIs worked, since serotonin function changed within hours of taking the drug, but depression didn't get better for about four weeks.

So, are antidepressants effective?

Even though Moncrieff and his colleagues' new paper doesn't say anything new, it does us all a favor by restating what has been clear for a while: there is no evidence to support the chemical imbalance theory. The article has gotten a lot of attention from the media, which has helped spread their message.

But many people, including the study's authors, have extrapolated from the study's results to say that it shows that antidepressants don't work, which isn't true. It has often been found that a treatment works before figuring out how it accomplishes that.

Many common medicines, such as aspirin, morphine, and penicillin, were used for decades before we knew how they worked. Knowing that they worked made it possible to figure out how they worked, and this led to the development of new treatments.

The evidence that SSRIs work for depression is strong, as they consistently work better than placebos. Some argue that the difference between the drugs and the placebos isn't big enough to justify using them.

We still don't know exactly how or why antidepressants work. But we also don't fully understand how general anesthetics work. That isn't a good enough reason to stop the use of anesthetics.

Many people with depression feel better when they pay attention to their diet, exercise, and sleep. Psychotherapy can also be a big help. But even after trying these things, a lot of people still have trouble with depression. For them, antidepressants may be the best option available. It may take some time to find the right antidepressant for you. It takes a tremendous amount of patience and will to continue, but millions of people have found great relief from this process.

Chapter 13: Bad Habits

There are a number of things you do every day that can lower your serotonin levels. If you cut back on these things, you can feel better all around. If you've been having problems like anxiety, depression, feeling tired, having trouble sleeping, or forgetting things, you might want to make some changes to your daily routine. Here are six things you do every day that could cause your serotonin levels to drop.

1. Too much time spent on the couch

Some binge-watching of TV is good for the soul, but if you do it every day, it could lower your serotonin levels. Multiple studies have shown that exercise both makes and releases more serotonin. This means that if you don't move around much, you may have less of this neurotransmitter. In fact, exercise works better than a prescription drug that aims to boost serotonin over the long term.

2. Staying Inside

Not everyone likes to be outside, but if you spend too much time inside, your serotonin levels can go down because sunlight is a good source of the neurotransmitter. Not getting enough sunlight can make it hard to focus, make you feel bad, and make you lose interest in everyday things.

3. Not Having a Well-Rounded Diet

Your diet affects how you feel, and not getting enough carbs, fermented foods, or B vitamins can cause your serotonin levels to drop. B vitamins act as "activators" that turn amino acids in your food into the neurotransmitter serotonin. If you eat a lot of vegetables and whole fruits, you'll make sure you get a lot of these B vitamins, like folate, which is found in spinach and other vegetables. Foods that are high in probiotics can help keep your gut healthy.

4. How Much Coffee You Drink

Even though caffeine can give you a much-needed energy boost, you can have too much of a good thing. A cup of coffee can temporarily raise the amount of serotonin in our bodies, but if you drink too much caffeine and become addicted to it, the withdrawal from caffeine can cause a serious lack of serotonin.

5. Skipping Out On Sleep

Not getting enough sleep can make you feel tired, but it can also stop your body from making serotonin. A study found that serotonin receptors become less sensitive over time when people don't get enough sleep. This makes you more likely to get disorders like depression, so it's important to get enough sleep every night.

6. Not Being Present

Letting your mind wander to worries about the future might not seem like a big deal, but it can make us sad. Research shows that mindfulness raises dopamine and serotonin levels, but the opposite is also true. Cortisol levels can stay too high if we don't take time to just be. And when our cortisol levels are too high for too long, cortisol goes around eating serotonin like Pac Man eats ghosts.

Getting rid of these habits can help keep your serotonin levels steady so you can feel happy and energized.

Did this book help you in some way? If so, I'd love to hear about it. Honest reviews help readers find the right book for their needs. Follow this link to leave a review.

If you enjoyed this book, you may also enjoy:

The Dopamine Book: How to Maximize Dopamine Levels Naturally

The Sleep Book: How to Maximize Your Body's Ability to Sleep Naturally

How to Make the Bad Feelings Go Away

Follow the author on Instagram for free book giveaways (no strings attached), free mental health information, and more:

References

Ruscio, D. M. (2022, November 21). *Foods that boost serotonin: The impact on Gut & Brain Health*. Dr. Michael Ruscio, DC. Retrieved March 10, 2023, from https://drruscio.com/foods-that-boost-serotonin/

Serotonin: What is it, Function & Levels. Cleveland Clinic. (n.d.). Retrieved March 10, 2023, from https://my.clevelandclinic.org/health/articles/22572-serotonin

Gotter, A. (2018, September 29). *What is tryptophan? uses, benefits, and foods*. Healthline. Retrieved March 14, 2023, from https://www.healthline.com/health/tryptophan#common-uses

Young, S. N. (2007, November). *How to increase serotonin in the human brain without drugs*. Journal of psychiatry & neuroscience : JPN. Retrieved March 14, 2023, from https://www.ncbi.nlm.nih.gov/pmc/articles/PMC2077351/

Collins, H. M. (2020, April 10). *Chronic isolation and serotonin: How social distancing can affect the brain*. Medium. Retrieved March 14, 2023, from https://helencollins1996.medium.com/chronic-isolation-and-serotonin-how-social-distancing-can-affect-the-brain-84c54a2e25dd

By. (2018, May 3). *How does thinking positive thoughts affect neuroplasticity?* MeTEOR Education. Retrieved March 14, 2023, from https://meteoreducation.com/how-does-thinking-positive-thoughts-affect-neuroplasticity/

Borbely AA and Tobler I. (1989): Endogenous sleep-inducing substances and the control of sleep. Physiological Review 69:605–670

TimDeakin. (2017, April 10). *Serotonin vs melatonin the science behind a good night's sleep*. Mammoth Comfort. Retrieved March 14, 2023, from https://mammothcomfort.com/all-articles/melatonin-vs-serotonin-science-behind-good-nights-sleep/#:~:text=In%20short%2C%20melatonin%20helps%20you,feelings%20of%20depression%20and%20lethargy.

Melatonin dosage by age and weight. Sleep Foundation. (2023, March 10). Retrieved March 14, 2023, from https://www.sleepfoundation.org/melatonin/melatonin-dosage-how-much-should-you-take

EndurElite. (n.d.). *The Ultimate Guide on 5-HTP (Griffonia simplicifolia)*. EndurElite. Retrieved March 14, 2023, from https://endurelite.com/blogs/free-nutrition-supplement-and-training-articles-for-runners-and-cyclists/5-htp-griffonia-simplicifolia-uses-side-effects-interactions-and-dosage

Serotonin syndrome: What it is, causes, symptoms & treatment. Cleveland Clinic. (n.d.). Retrieved March 14, 2023, from https://my.clevelandclinic.org/heal

th/diseases/17687-serotonin-syndrome

Sheryl Ankrom, M. S. (2022, March 11). *Drugs that increase the risk of serotonin syndrome.* Verywell Mind. Retrieved March 14, 2023, from https://www.verywellmind.com/medications-and-serotonin-syndrome-2584342

Google. (n.d.). Google search. Retrieved March 15, 2023, from https://www.google.com/search?q=genetics%2Band%2Bserotonin&rlz=1C1CHBF_enUS881US881&oq=genetics%2Band%2Bserotonin&aqs=chrome..69i57.5531j0j4&sourceid=chrome&ie=UTF-8

Guardian News and Media. (2022, August 3). *The chemical imbalance theory of depression is dead – but that doesn't mean antidepressants don't work | Christopher Davey.* The Guardian. Retrieved March 15, 2023, from https://www.theguardian.com/commentisfree/2022/aug/03/the-chemical-imbalance-theory-of-depression-is-dead-but-that-doesnt-mean-antidepressants-dont-work

Scaccia, A. (2022, September 26). Serotonin: Functions, normal range, side effects, and more. Healthline. Retrieved March 15, 2023, from https://www.healthline.com/health/mental-health/serotonin

Made in United States
Troutdale, OR
02/14/2024

17674676R00086